straw

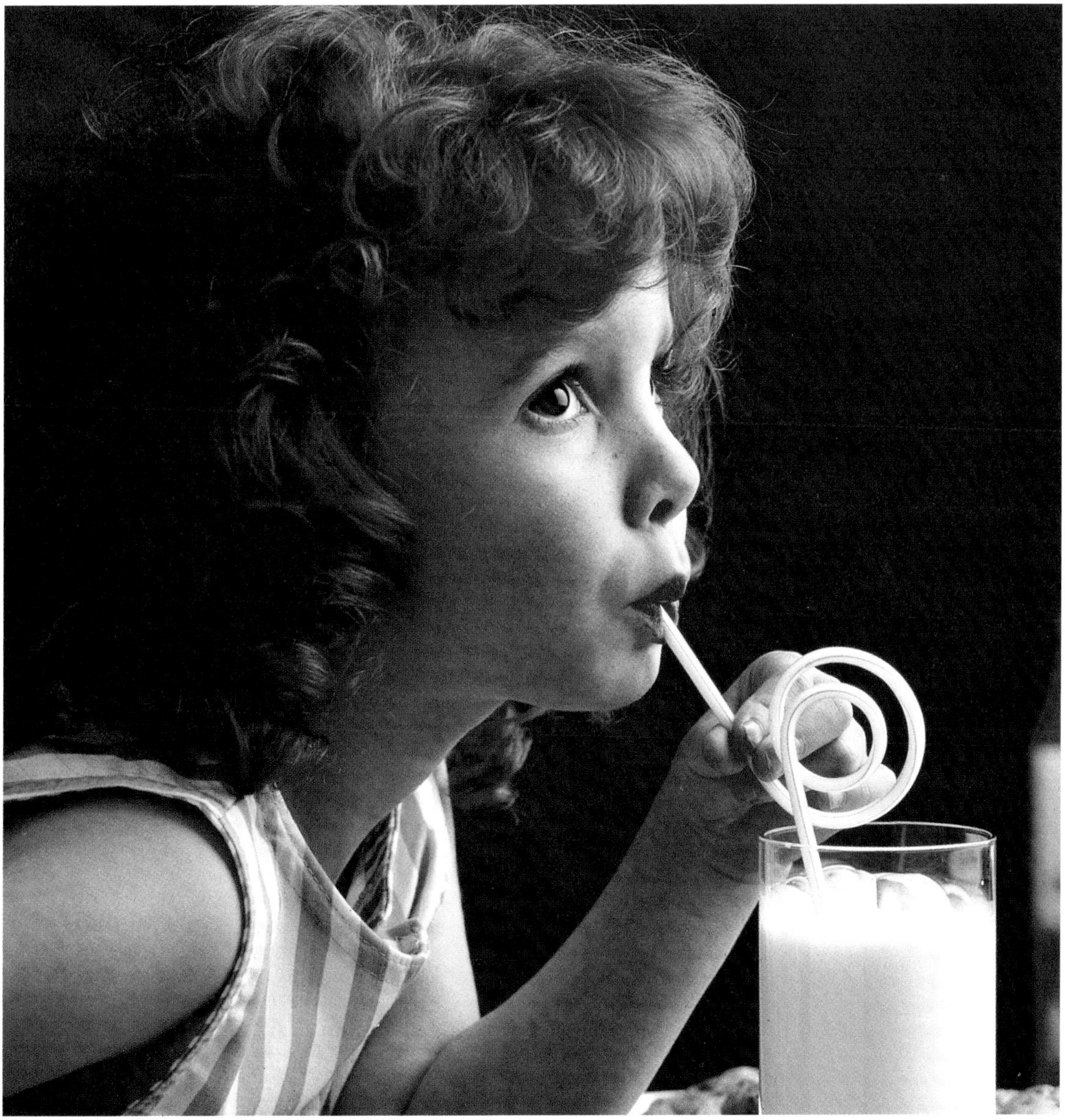

stripes

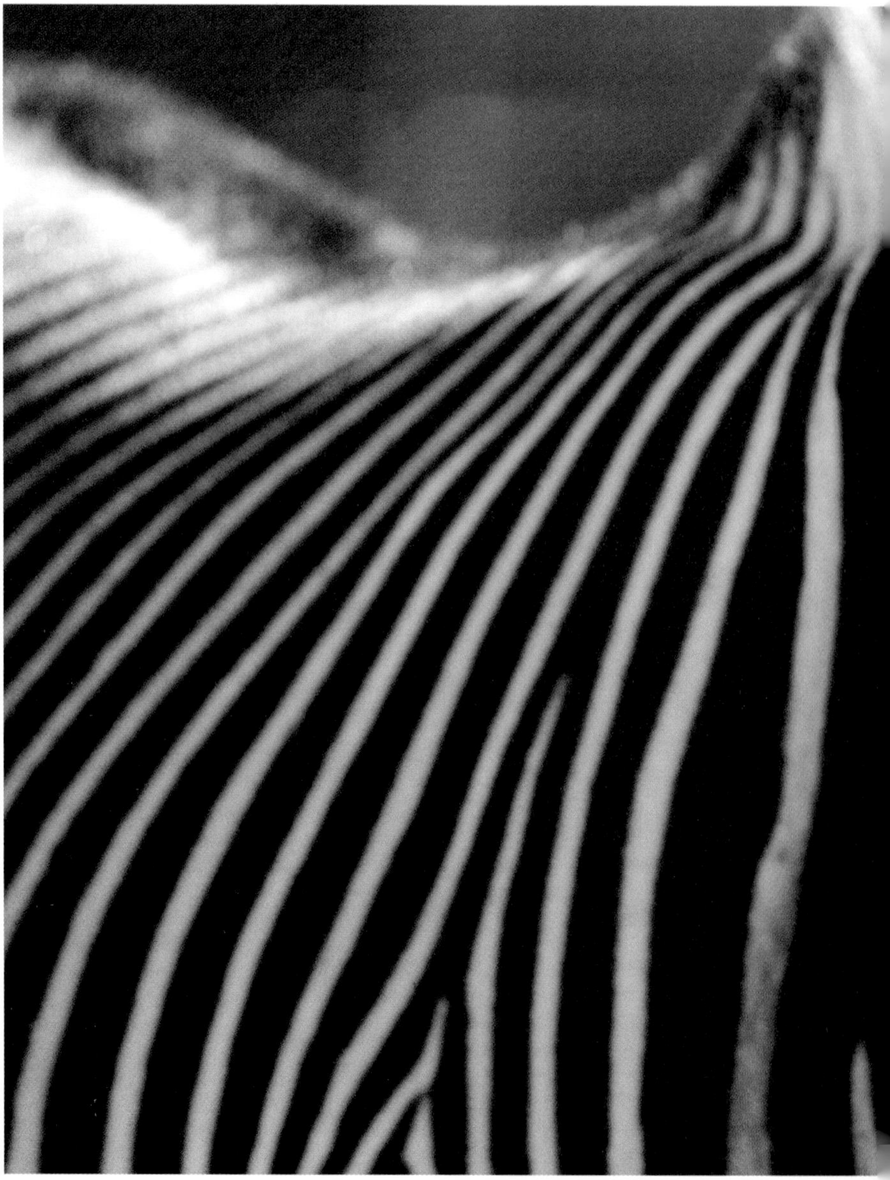

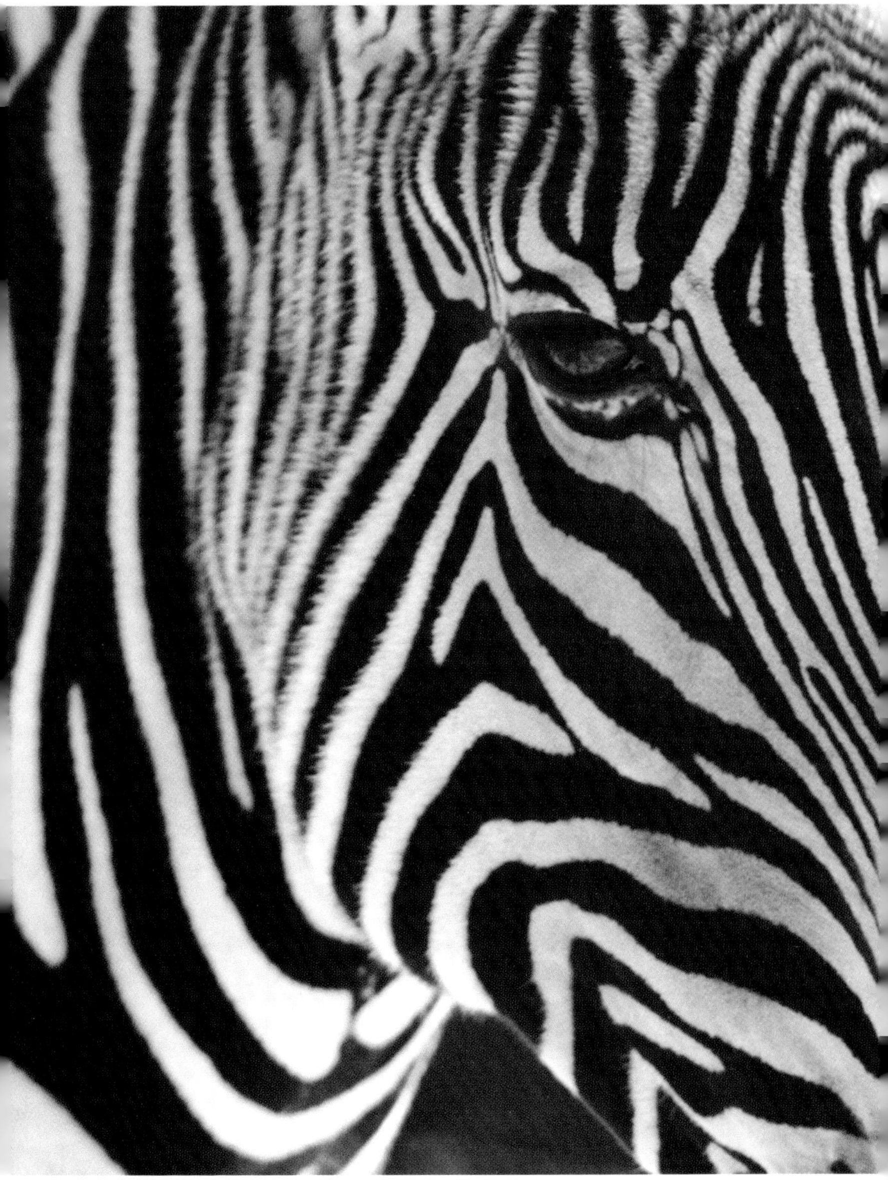

etch

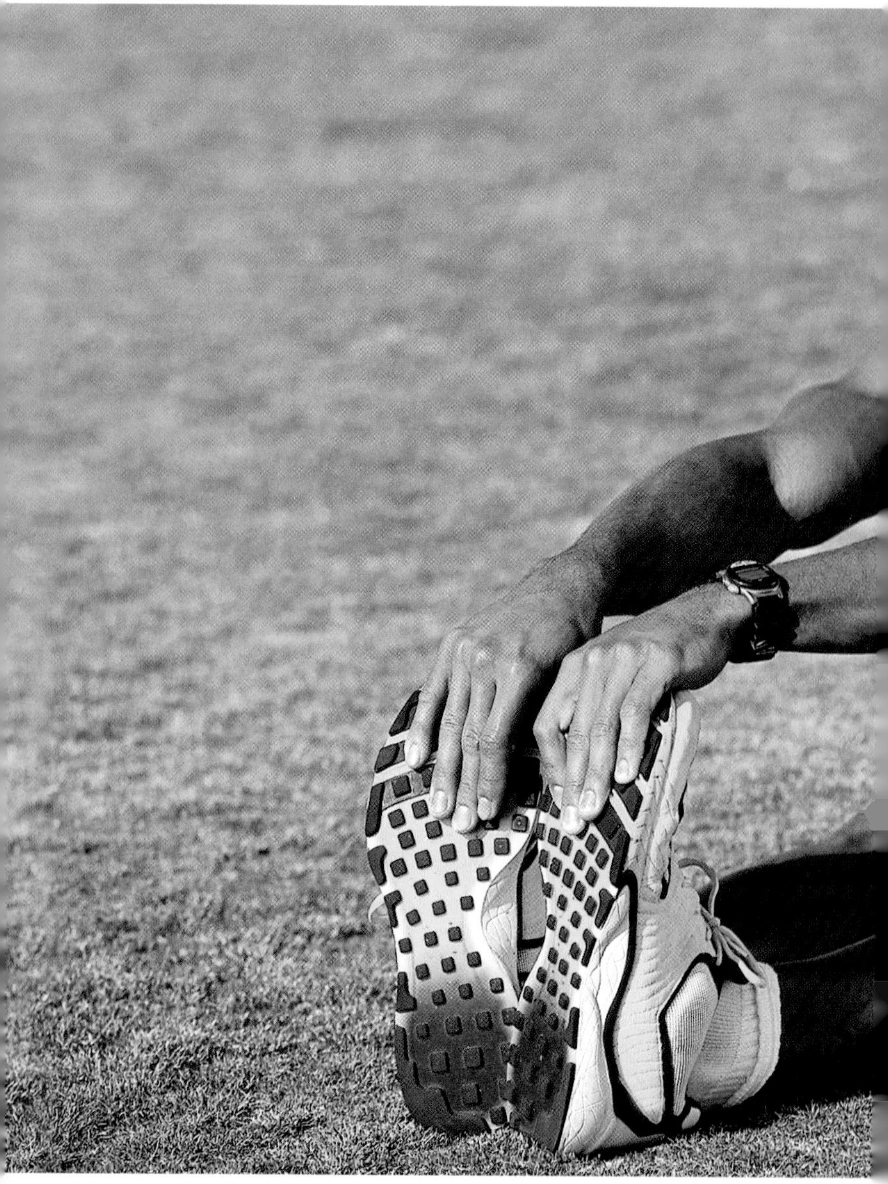

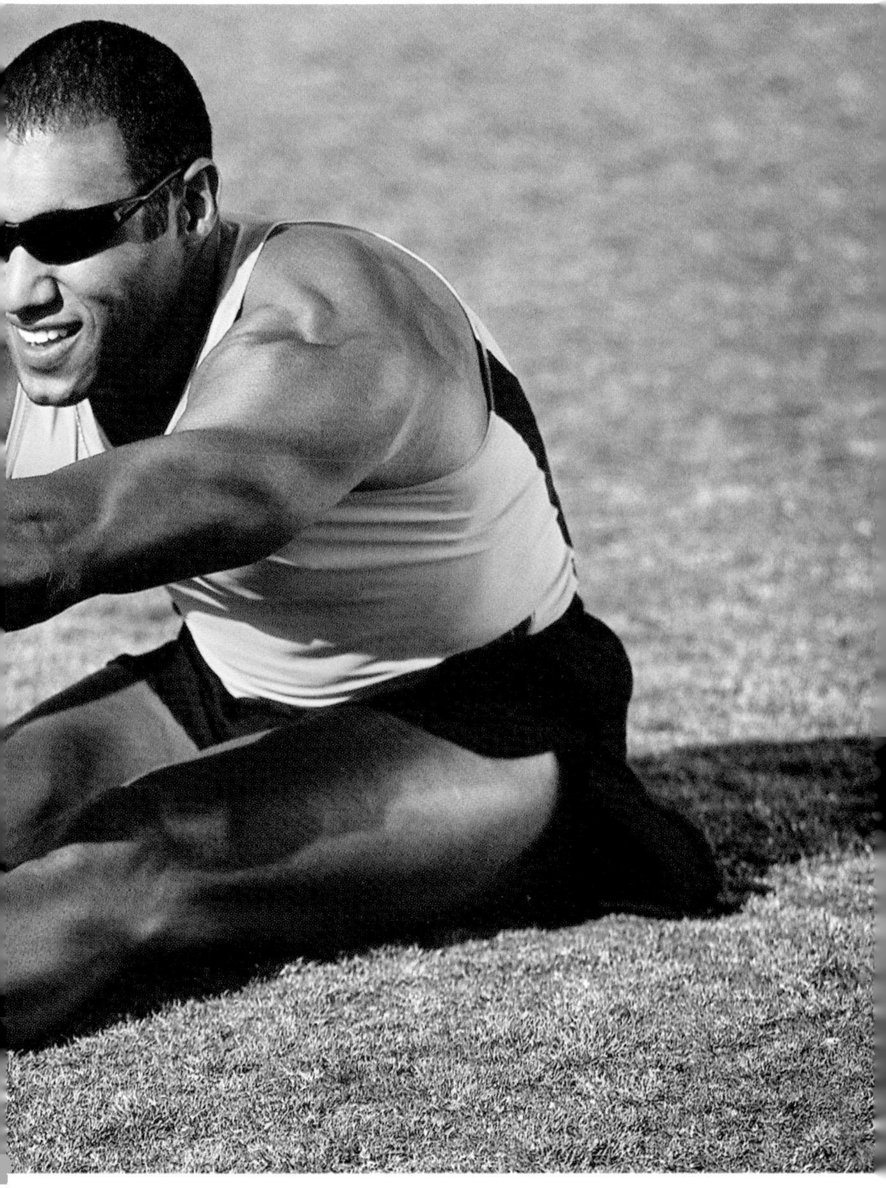

eet

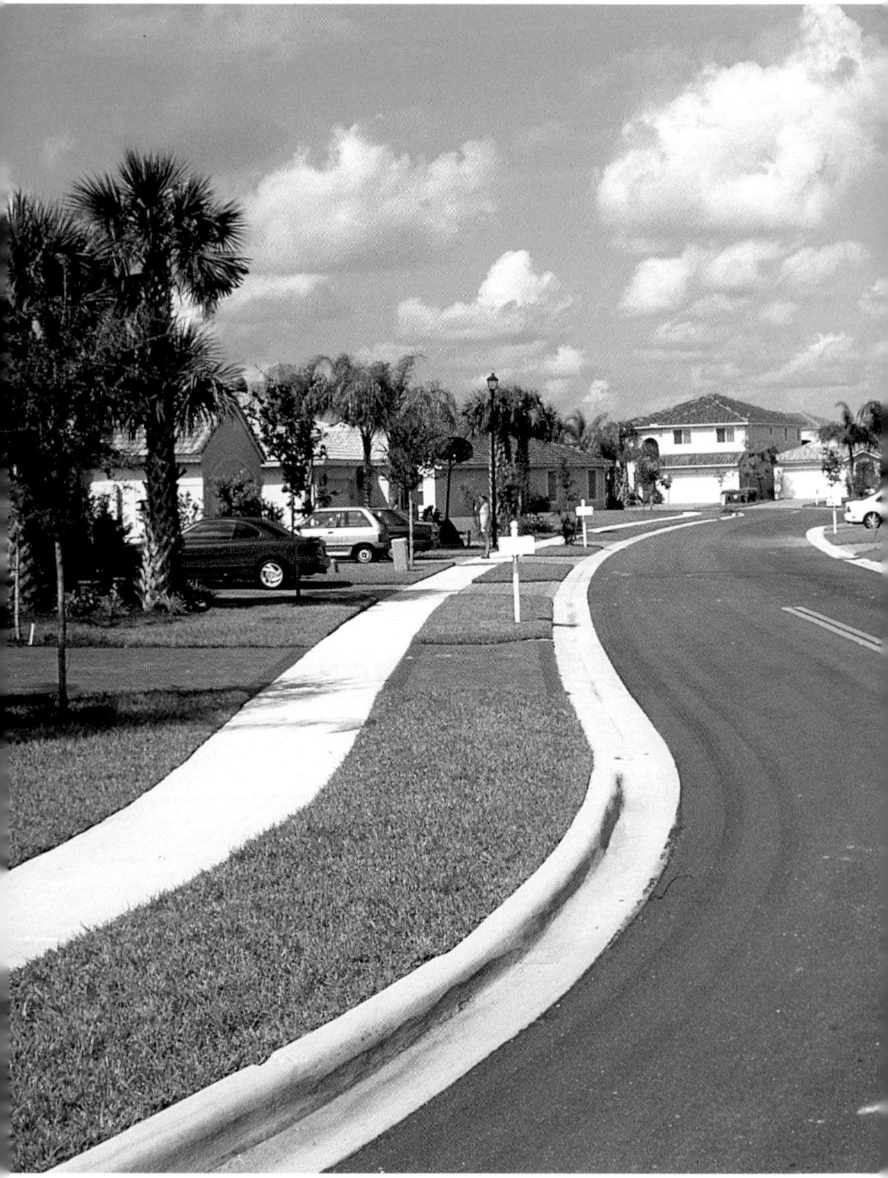

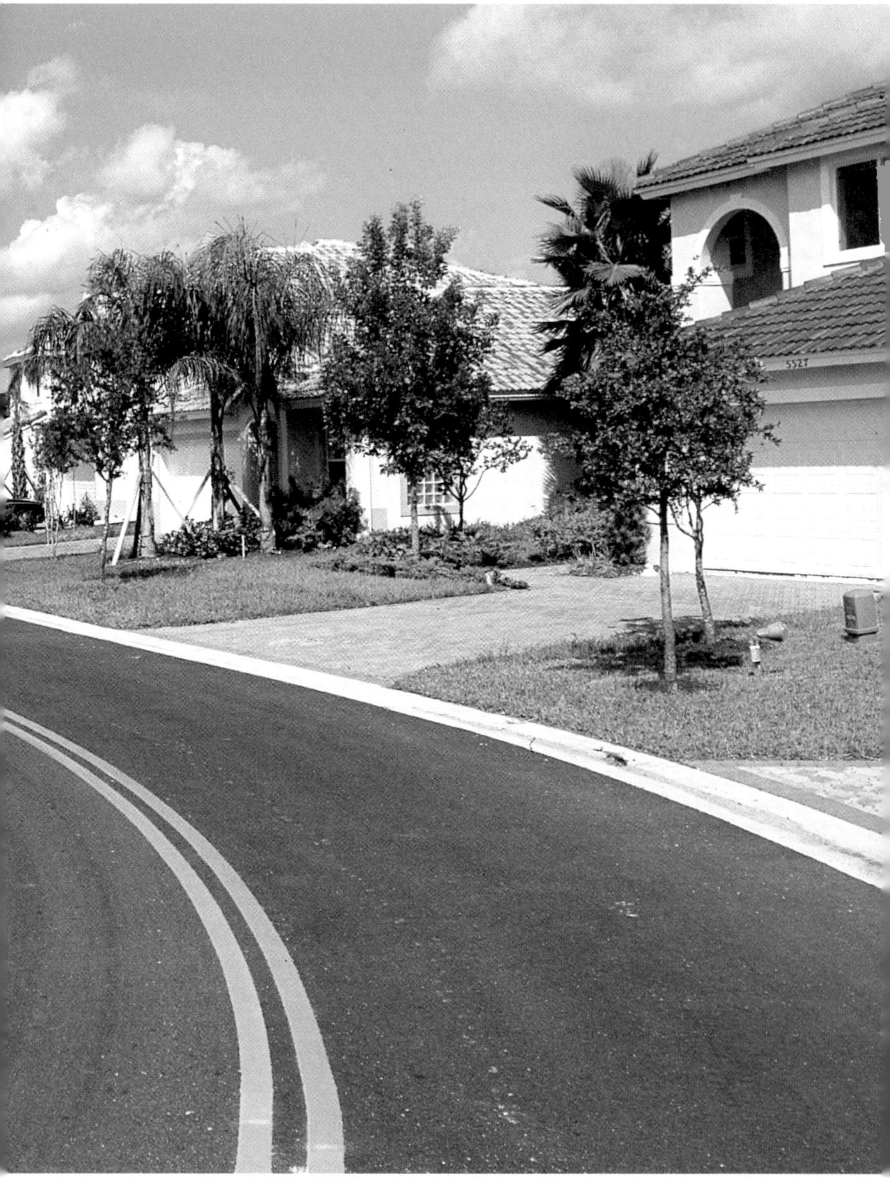
5527

ong

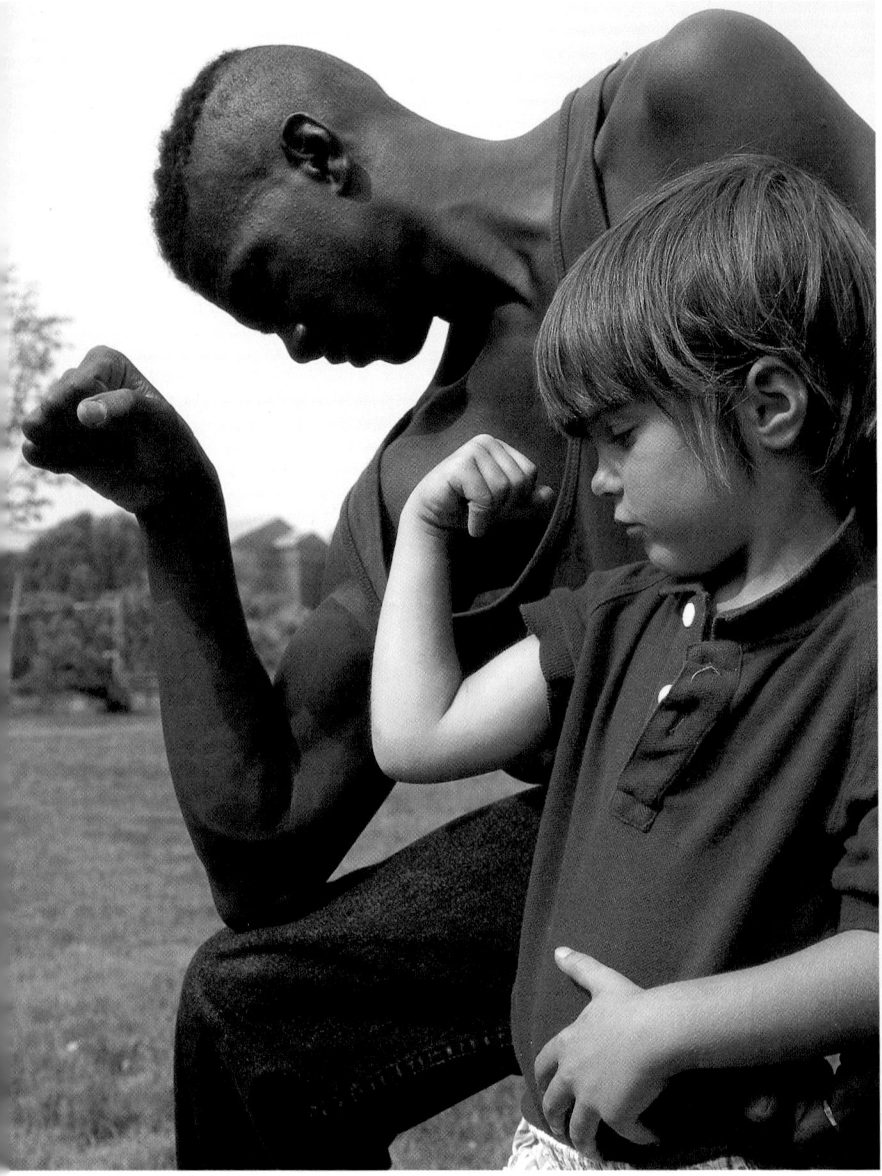